William Bolcom/Curtis Curtis-Smith

Collusions

Pieces for Solo Piano

Co-composed by
William Bolcom and Curtis Curtis-Smith

1. Get Up!

2. Moonlight on Ice

3. Snippets (Some Short, Some Long)

4. Sarabande Mortelle

5. Fuzzy Wuzzy's Serenade

ISBN: 978-1-4234-2704-9

EDWARD B. Marks Music COMPANY / EXCLUSIVELY DISTRIBUTED BY HAL•LEONARD® CORPORATION
7777 W. BLUEMOUND RD. P.O. BOX 13819 MILWAUKEE, WI 53213

Visit Hal Leonard Online at
www.halleonard.com

Facsimile of first manuscript page of *Collusions*.

DURATION: *ca.* 10'

Collusions

1. Get Up!

Curtis Curtis-Smith
& William Bolcom

2. Moonlight on Ice

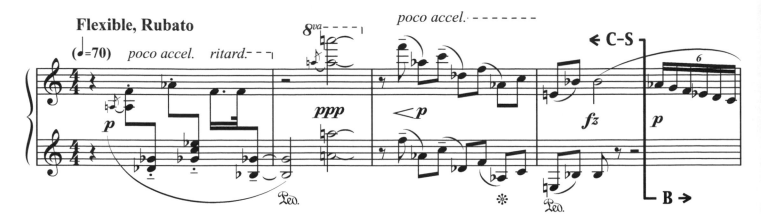

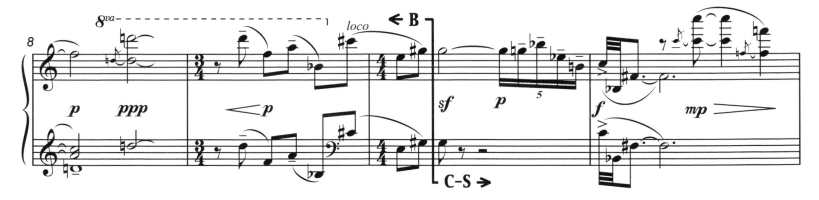

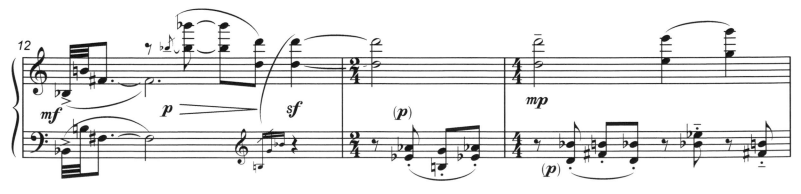

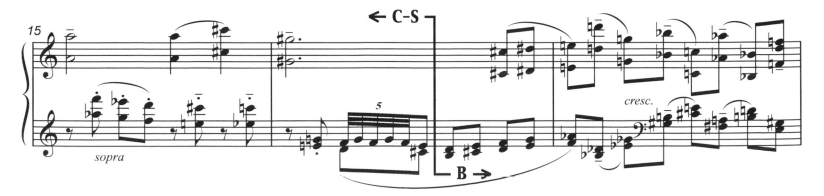

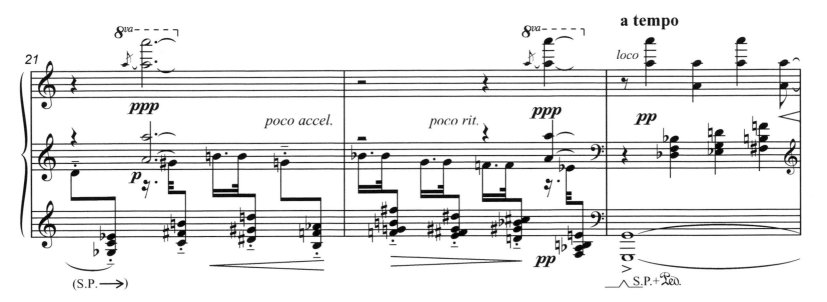

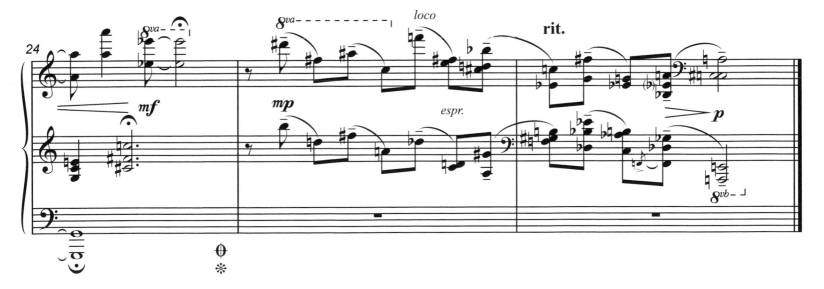

3. Snippets (Some Short, Some Long)

Play some of these short extracts in any order once through.

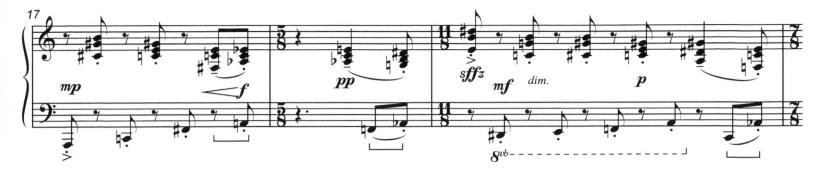

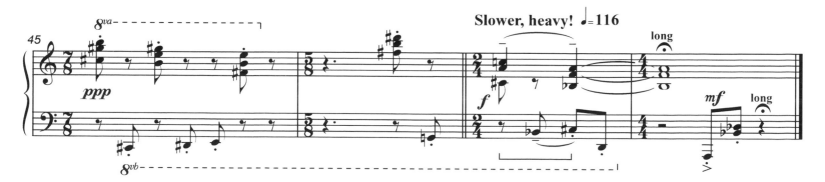

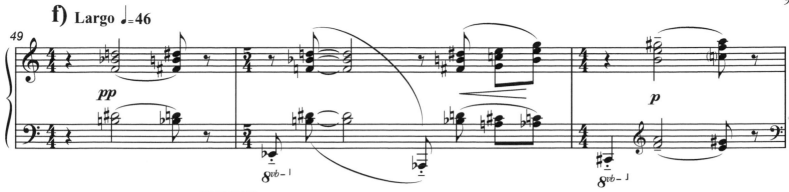

f) Largo ♩=46

Slower ♩=42   **ritard.**   ♩=36

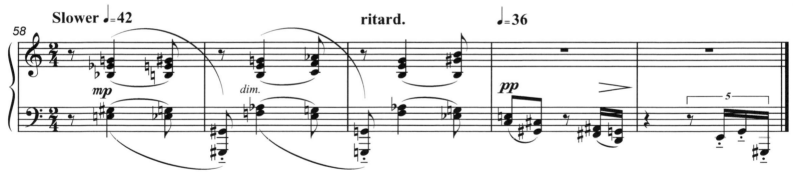

g) Slow Swing ♩=72

ritard.   **Tempo I**

4. Sarabande Mortelle

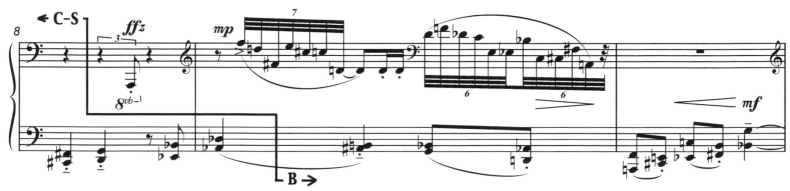

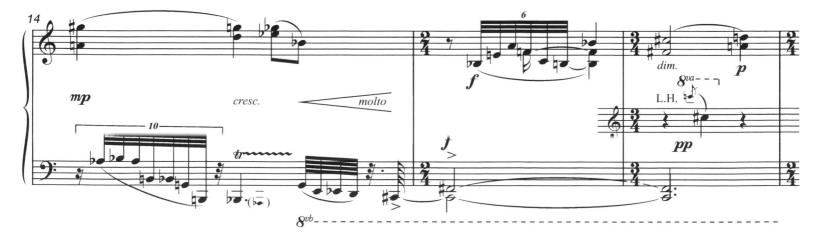

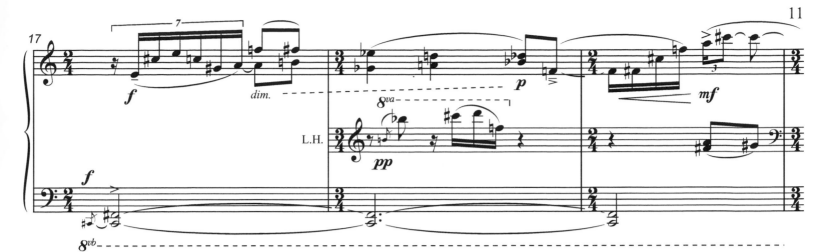

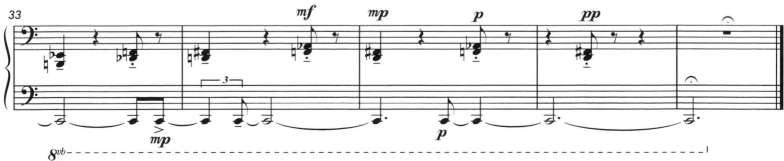

5. Fuzzy Wuzzy's Serenade

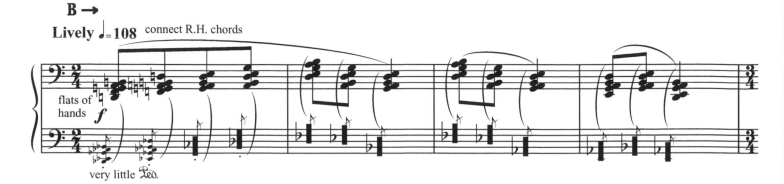

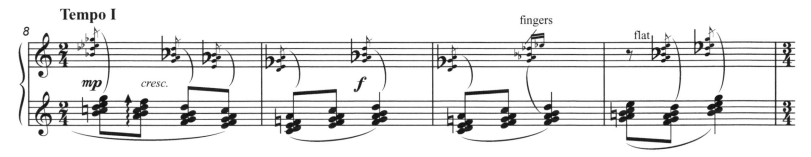

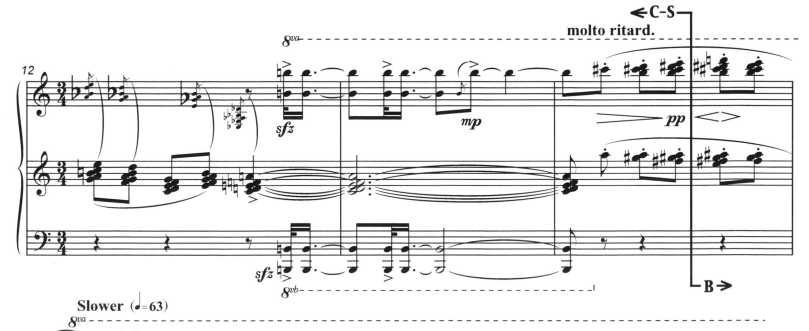

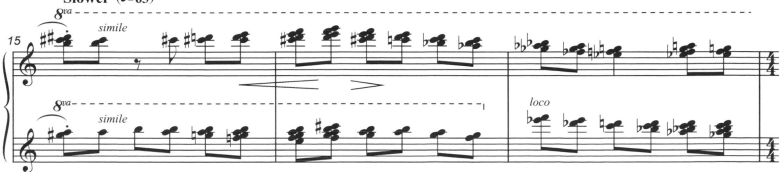

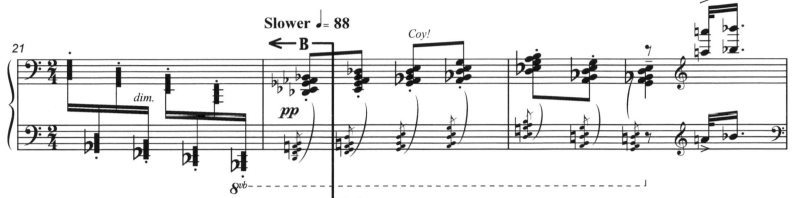

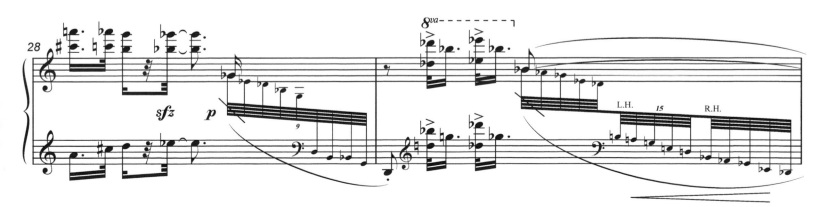

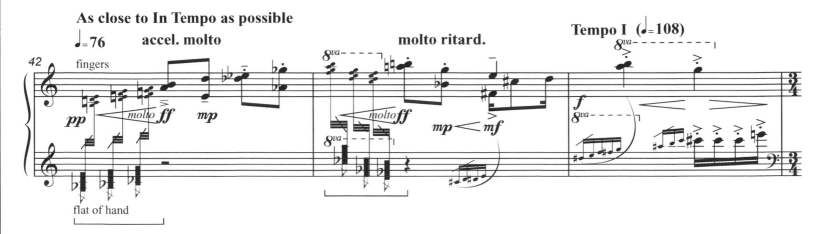

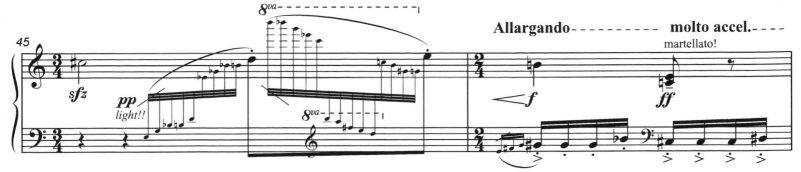

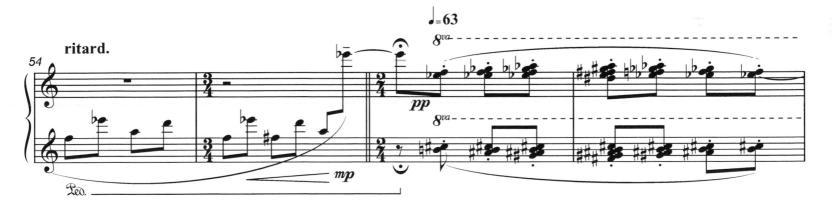

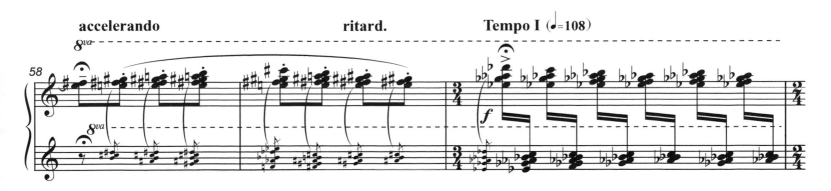

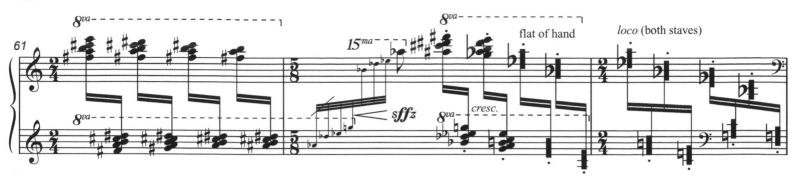

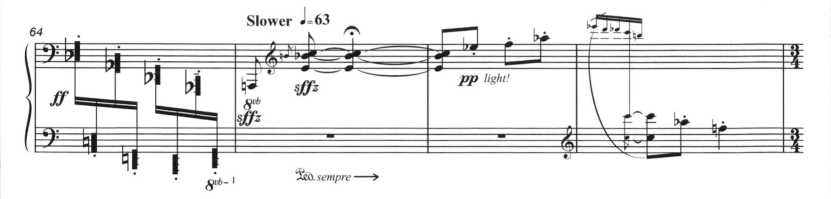

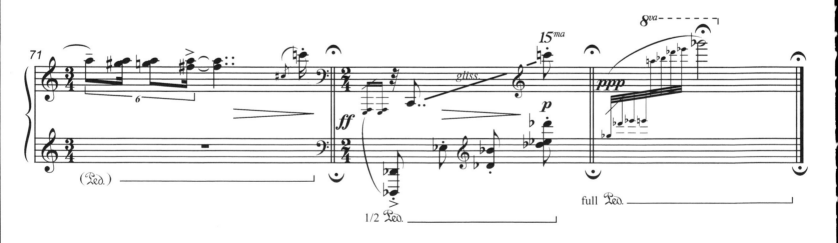